D1250740

STEM Projects in **MINECRAFT**®

The Unofficial Guide to
Studying Oceans in
MINECRAFT®

JILL KEPPELER

PowerKiDS press.

New York

Published in 2020 by The Rosen Publishing Group, Inc.
29 East 21st Street, New York, NY 10010

First Edition

Editor: Greg Roza
Book Design: Rachel Rising
Illustrator: Matías Lapegüe

Photo Credits: Cover, pp.1,3,4,6,8,10,12,14,16,18,20,22,23,24 (background) Shutterstock/Evgeniy Dzyuba; pp. 4,10,14,18,20 (inset) Levent Konuk/Shutterstock; p. 5 Naeblys/Shutterstock.com; p. 10 Eric Isselee/Shutterstock.com; p. 17 best works/Shutterstock.com; p. 18 Elena Schweitzer/Shutterstock.com; p. 22 Ljupco Smokovski/Shutterstock.com.

Cataloging-in-Publication Data

Names: Keppeler, Jill.
Title: The unofficial guide to studying oceans in Minecraft ® / Jill Keppeler.
Description: New York : PowerKids Press, 2020. | Series: STEM projects in Minecraft | Includes glossary and index.
Identifiers: ISBN 9781725310629 (pbk.) | ISBN 9781725310643 (library bound) | ISBN 9781725310636 (6 pack)
Subjects: LCSH: Oceanography–Juvenile literature. | Minecraft (Game) – Juvenile literature.
Classification: LCC GV1469.M55 K47 2020 | DDC 794.8–dc23

Manufactured in the United States of America

CPSIA Compliance Information: Batch #CW20PK. For Further Information contact Rosen Publishing, New York, New York at 1-800-237-9932.

Contents

Big Blue Biomes

Oceans and seas cover about 71 percent of Earth's surface. That's a lot of water! In the game of *Minecraft*, ocean **biomes** also cover a lot of the surface of the overworld—up to about a third of it. These big blue biomes hold many **resources**, many secrets—and many dangers.

Oceanography is the science that deals with the oceans, including their waters and their resources. You can be an oceanographer in *Minecraft*! There's a lot to learn and discover. However, you need to be prepared. There are tools you can use to breathe underwater and ways to deal with the dangers you'll find there.

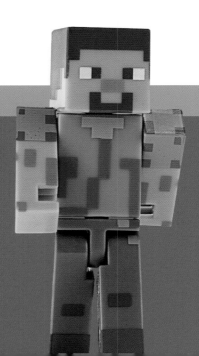

MINECRAFT MANIA

If you're going to explore the oceans in *Minecraft,* you'll need to find a way to breathe. You can only stay underwater for so long before your oxygen bar will empty and you'll start to drown.

Oceans on Earth are filled with salt water. However, there's no difference between salt water and fresh water in *Minecraft*.

Our Oceans

On Earth, there are five main oceans, although they run together. These are the Pacific, Atlantic, Indian, Arctic, and Southern Oceans. There are also many seas and gulfs.

There are nine ocean types in *Minecraft*. Regular oceans are about 20 blocks deep. The seafloor is often made of gravel. Varieties have different climates, and thus different sea life and features. There are frozen oceans, which have a surface covered mainly with ice; cold oceans; **lukewarm** oceans; and warm oceans. Most of these (except for warm oceans) also have a deep version, which can be more than 30 blocks deep.

<- - polar bear

MINECRAFT MANIA

You can't feel temperature in *Minecraft* biomes, but you can see the signs of it. Different temperature biomes, including oceans, have different life-forms and differently colored grass, leaves, and water.

Frozen ocean biomes can have icebergs.
Polar bears often **spawn** in these biomes.

There are ways to extend your breathing time underwater in *Minecraft*. You can put a respiration, or breathing, **enchantment** on a helmet. You can also make a **potion** of water breathing that lasts for three or eight minutes. If you have a turtle-shell helmet, you have 10 seconds of extra breathing time every time you duck underwater.

If you find a heart of the sea and eight nautilus shells, you can make a conduit. Once a conduit is activated underwater in a frame of prismarine blocks, you'll be able to breathe underwater in a range around it. The range depends on how big the frame is.

MINECRAFT MANIA

To make a turtle-shell helmet, you need five scutes. In *Minecraft*, scutes are pieces of shell dropped by baby turtles as they grow into adults.

Conduit frames are made of 16 to 42 blocks of prismarine, a stone you can find in ocean monuments in *Minecraft*. The conduit itself needs to be fully surrounded by water.

Fish in the Sea

Many **aquatic** plants and mobs, or moving creatures, live below the surface of the water in *Minecraft*. Seagrass is found in most ocean biomes, as well as in swamps and rivers. It can be one or two blocks tall. Kelp also grows in most oceans, usually near seagrass. It can grow very tall—up to 26 blocks if there's enough ocean above it.

There are four kinds of fish in *Minecraft*: salmon, cod, pufferfish, and **tropical** fish. You can catch and eat cod and salmon. Pufferfish puff up and will poison you if you get too close to them!

MINECRAFT MANIA

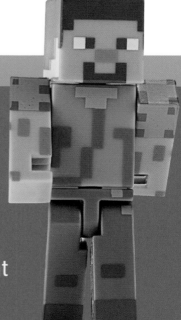

Kelp, a kind of seaweed, can be very useful in both real life and *Minecraft*. In the game, if you dry kelp pieces in a furnace, you can then eat them. Or, you can combine nine pieces of dried kelp into a block and use that as fuel.

Tropical fish in *Minecraft* are only found in warm oceans. There are more than 3,000 kinds!

11

More than Fish

Minecraft oceans may also contain dolphins, turtles, and squid. Squid don't do much other than swim around. Turtles may be found both on land and in water. They dig nests and lay eggs on warm beaches. Like real sea turtles, they always go back to their home beach to lay eggs.

Dolphins swim in Minecraft oceans in groups. They squeal and chirp and jump out of the water. They need air just like real-world dolphins and can drown without it. Dolphins won't usually hurt players, but if a player hurts a dolphin, that dolphin and all others in the area will attack.

MINECRAFT MANIA

There are hostile mobs in Minecraft oceans, too. Drowned are zombies that spawn in the water, although they may go onto land at night. Some drowned carry tridents, a weapon they can throw at players.

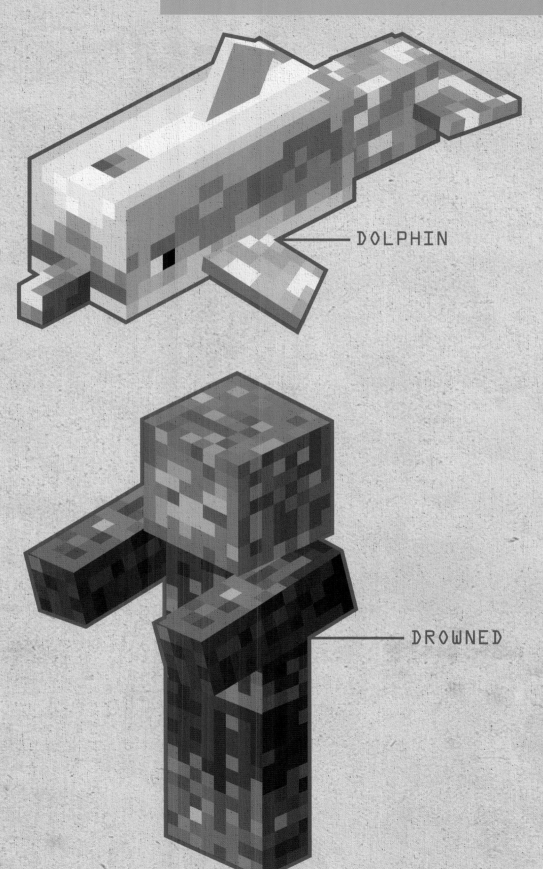

DOLPHIN

DROWNED

Coral Reefs

Coral reefs are ridges formed in warm, shallow oceans by tiny creatures called corals. There are coral reefs in *Minecraft*, too. Colorful coral blocks and coral fans make up these areas in warm ocean biomes.

Minecraft coral comes in five different colors and five different varieties. Living coral is brightly colored, but any kind of coral dies when it's moved out of water. Dead coral is a flat gray color. This reflects coral bleaching in the real world. This is when the tiny creatures living on coral leave or die, which makes the coral white. Bleached coral often dies.

<-- - **coral fan**

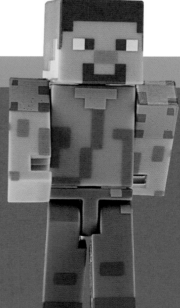

MINECRAFT MANIA

Sea pickles live in *Minecraft* coral reefs. They grow in small colonies and give off light. There are real-life sea pickles too! They're pyrosomes, strange animals that usually live in tropical waters.

A healthy coral reef has many creatures, just like a *Minecraft* reef. However, increasing ocean temperatures have been hurting many real-world coral reefs.

Ravines

Even in areas without coral reefs, *Minecraft's* ocean bottoms aren't just flat and featureless. There are hills and valleys and caves. Sometimes, there are ravines. These deep cracks in the ocean floor are very long and very deep, sometimes all the way down to **bedrock**.

Ocean ravines often have **magma** blocks at their bottom. These glowing blocks will hurt you if you step on them. They also produce bubble columns, which will pull players and items downward. These columns can go all the way to the surface. They're very dangerous, but an underwater player can also refill their air supply in them—if they're careful!

MINECRAFT MANIA

You can travel over a *Minecraft* ocean's surface in a boat. However, bubble columns will pull a boat downward, too, even if a player is in it.

Underwater ravines may also be called **trenches**. The deepest point in Earth's ocean is the Mariana Trench in the Pacific Ocean. It goes down to 36,000 feet (10,972.8 m) deep!

HIGHEST AND DEEPEST POINTS ON EARTH

MOUNT EVEREST

MARIANA TRENCH

You can also find mysterious underwater ruins at the bottom of *Minecraft* oceans. These ruins may have one small building or a group of many buildings. The buildings, which are mostly made of stone bricks or sandstone, might be just a few blocks or they might be nearly complete.

Look closely if you find underwater ruins. Many buildings will have a hidden chest that contains loot. This loot may include a buried treasure map. If you travel to the location marked by a red "X" on the map and dig, you'll find another chest filled with treasure, including a heart of the sea.

MINECRAFT MANIA

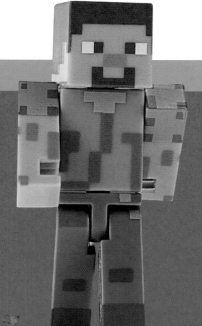

You can also find shipwrecks in *Minecraft*. Most shipwrecks are underwater, although you can also find them on beaches. Sometimes, the ship's masts poke up above the water's surface.

Monumental

The biggest structure you'll find in deep *Minecraft* oceans doesn't have a real-life match at all. Ocean monuments are huge underwater buildings made of prismarine, a blue-green stone. They have many rooms, including one where you can find eight golden blocks.

It's not easy to get this treasure, though. Hostile mobs called guardians spawn in and around ocean monuments. Each monument also has three elder guardians, which are even harder to beat and can hit you with an enchantment that keeps you from mining the precious prismarine or gold. Do you have what it takes to **raid** an ocean monument? Good luck!

MINECRAFT MANIA

Ocean monuments are the only place in *Minecraft* where you can find sponges. You can dry sponges in a furnace and use them to remove water from areas.

21

Making Mods

You can make your *Minecraft* creations even more exciting with modifications, or mods. Using a computer program called ScriptCraft, you can create new blocks, change the way the game functions, and make your own games. Imagine what you could create! Would you like to add blue whales to your *Minecraft* oceans? What about mermaids?

If you're interested in learning how to create mods in *Minecraft*, visit the website below. You'll find the information needed to get started with ScriptCraft and build your own *Minecraft* mods.

https://scriptcraftjs.org/

Glossary

aquatic: Living in the water or related to something that lives in the water.

bedrock: The solid rock under the surface of Earth. In *Minecraft*, the layer of special rock that lies at the bottom of a *Minecraft* world.

biome: A natural community of plants and animals, such as a forest or desert.

enchantment: A magic spell. In *Minecraft*, a spell you can place on an item.

laser: A device that produces a narrow beam of light or the beam itself.

lukewarm: Slightly warm.

magma: Hot, liquid, or soft rock below the surface of Earth.

potion: A drink meant to have a special effect on someone.

raid: To carry out a sudden attack.

resource: Something that can be used.

spawn: To bring forth. In video games, when characters suddenly appear in a certain place.

trench: A long, narrow hole in the ground.

tropical: Warm and wet.

Index

B
boats, 13, 16
bubble columns, 16
buried treasure map, 18, 19

C
cod, 10
conduit, 8, 9
coral reef, 14, 15, 16

D
dolphins, 12, 13
drowned, 12, 13

E
elder guardians, 20

G
guardians, 20

H
heart of the sea, 8, 18

K
kelp, 10

M
magma blocks, 16

N
nautilus shells, 8

O
ocean monument, 9, 20, 21

P
prismarine, 8, 9, 20
pufferfish, 10

R
ravines, 16, 17
ruins, 18

S
salmon, 10
seagrass, 10
sea pickles, 14
shipwrecks, 18, 19
sponges, 21
squid, 12

T
tropical fish, 10, 11
turtle, 8, 12

Websites

Due to the changing nature of Internet links, PowerKids Press has developed an online list of websites related to the subject of this book. This site is updated regularly. Please use this link to access the list:
www.powerkidslinks.com/stemmc/oceans